ANGELS

ANGELS

David Pawson

Anchor Recordings

First published in Great Britain in 2015 by
Anchor Recordings Ltd
72 The Street, Kennington, Ashford TN24 9HS

**For more of David Pawson's teaching,
including DVDs and CDs, go to
www.davidpawson.com**

**FOR FREE DOWNLOADS
www.davidpawson.org**

**For further information, email
info@davidpawsonministry.com**

ISBN 978 1 909886 02 5

Printed by Lightning Source

`

Contents

This book is based on a series of talks. Originating as it does from the spoken word, its style will be found by many readers to be somewhat different from my usual written style. It is hoped that this will not detract from the substance of the biblical teaching found here.

As always, I ask the reader to compare everything I say or write with what is written in the Bible and, if at any point a conflict is found, always to rely upon the clear teaching of scripture.

David Pawson

PROLOGUE

A friend and I were driving back to Basingstoke late one night in a heavy snowstorm. By the time we reached the town, the roads were packed snow, covered in ice. In our 4x4 we passed many abandoned vehicles (over a thousand in the area, we later learned). But even our 4-wheel drive failed to climb the last hill before my home. A couple of empty cars lay at the foot of a sheet of pure ice. We managed to get half way up before the tyres completely failed to grip and we slid to a standstill.

Suddenly I became aware of someone standing just outside the window (I was in the passenger seat), and when I lowered the glass he told us he would help us out of our predicament! He then gave my friend, who was driving, very precise instructions ("foot off the accelerator, steer over to the right, now the left," etc.). He stayed with us until we were able to reach the top of the hill and coast down to my home.

It was only then that I realised how extraordinary his intervention had been. Our headlights had picked out no-one on the road, only the few deserted vehicles at the foot of the hill. He had suddenly appeared at our side and as abruptly disappeared before we could thank him. More significantly, he had stayed next to us while on a steep slope covered in ice, up which it would have been difficult, if not impossible, for anyone to stand, never mind move sideways. And he must have been exceptionally tall since I had to peer up through the window at him from a seat in a high vehicle. I have a vivid recollection of a dark, handsome face.

All this convinced me that it was yet another of the rare occasions in my life when I have been aware of a "guardian" angel and his timely assistance. Whether you, my reader, have had such an experience or not, there is enough information about angels in the Bible to prepare you for the day when you will be surrounded by the good ones in heaven or the bad ones in hell. Read on to find the difference.

1

GOOD ANGELS

First of all, please read 2 Kings 6:1–23. It is a most extraordinary account, and if I was not a Christian I would not believe it but it is a marvellous narrative, telling of how enemies became friends. I wonder what you think is the most wonderful thing in that passage — the axe floating, or the blindness, or just the fact that the Syrians never came raiding Israel again after their treatment.

Secondly, please now read Hebrews 1:1–2:9. That passage puts the angels in their place, us in our place, and Jesus in his place.

This topic of angels is commonly associated with Christmas and the birth narratives in the Gospels. There are nativity plays, and Christmas cards arrive, often featuring angels. There are little "angels" who are not always little angels in those nativity plays, and we shall be facing this subject. When we read the account in Luke's Gospel, we discover that the angels are an integral part of the record.

Right at the beginning, there is an angel announcing to Zechariah that he was going to have a little boy called John in his old age. Then you turn the pages and you find an angel coming to Mary (probably a fifteen-year old girl) and saying, "Even though you are not married you are going to have a baby boy." Then to her fiancé – a young man who was working hard as a carpenter to get enough money to set up home together – the same angel came and explained a most delicate situation and told Joseph that his fiancée was to have a baby. Then, after the baby was born, the baby should not have survived two years, humanly speaking, because the baby was so hated by a king that soldiers were sent to slaughter every child under two years in the entire district. It was an angel who came to Joseph again by night and said, "Joseph, get away to Egypt and take the boy with you."

The whole account is full of angels, yet I suppose that when we take down the fairy lights, put the decorations away and recycle the Christmas cards, many of us will put angels out of our thinking for another twelve months. Even if we take angels seriously over Christmas, there are some people, even churchgoers, who hardly ever consider that the angels are real. The typical debate between one Christmas and the next seems to resolve itself into a rather crude question as to whether somewhere out in the universe there is intelligent life. Whenever I hear people discussing this, I want to laugh and to tell them that the Bible said, two thousand years ago, that we are not the only intelligent beings in the universe – we are limited to earth, but out there are myriads of intelligent beings. The universe is not empty, it might look empty to our telescopes, but it is not really empty.

It is interesting that science fiction comes up with grotesque creatures that have far more mineral, animal and vegetable connections than spiritual, and weird creatures cross our screens in films and videos. One of the first Russian astronauts who went into space was asked by reporters, "What did you see up there?" He replied, "Well I didn't see any angels," and threw back his head and roared with laughter as he drank his vodka. But they saw him. It is laughable when people dismiss the angels as fairies, as creatures of childhood fantasy that you can leave behind with Santa Claus.

When we turn to the Bible, we find a very different attitude. From the first book to the last you will discover that angels are part of what happened. I will go so far as to say that I doubt if anybody can be a full Christian who doesn't believe in angels because, to put it very simply, in my mind a full Christian is someone who follows Jesus. Jesus believed in angels, and he had dealings with them, and he told us what to think about them, and he talked to us about them. How can I claim to follow Jesus and never give a serious thought to the angels who meant so much to him?

Before we try to answer the questions about who they are, what they are, what they look like, what they do, why the Bible tells us about them and whether it is of any practical help to me to know about angels, I must first clear the decks. Before you can build, you have to clear the site of anything standing there that shouldn't be. So let me deal with three wrong ideas, which I have encountered. One concerns the *appearance* of angels—what they look like. We must get out of our heads the idea that angels are beautiful creatures with long white nighties and beautifully fair, curly hair and blue eyes, wings and so on. There are some elements of truth in this and maybe they look a little like this when we see them in heaven, but this kind of "fairy" appearance is such that nobody could ever have entertained an angel unawares; and the Bible does say quite simply that some people have done so. Without realising it, they have had an angel in their home. Well, certainly if you opened your front door and there was a vision of that sort in front of you, there would be no doubts at all. Abraham and Lot were both visited by angels and did not realise at first that they were dealing with supernatural beings. Angels came in the simple form of human beings; they can appear that way.

Secondly, I want to deal with a wrong idea of their *origin*. They are not people who have died and turned into angels the other side of the grave. The Bible never gives any ground whatever for thinking that we become angels when we die.

I found this idea particularly rooted in connection with children, as if little children turn into angels and cherubs if they die. No, let us get it quite straight. The angels and human beings are quite separate, and have no such direct connection with each other. They were created separately; they are different orders of being, and the angels will never become human beings, nor will the human beings ever actually become angels.

Thirdly, let us look at their *function*. They are not mediators between man and God. They are not to be worshipped or prayed to. At least twice in the last book in the Bible, angels tell John, "Don't fall down and worship me. I am just a servant of God as you are." We are not to confuse angels with anything other than messengers of God. They are simply his messengers, to take his words, to do his bidding wherever they go. There was a craze at one stage in England (as there was elsewhere) for churches to claim saints or angels, and so we get all the names—Gabriel and St Michael were among the favourites.

Some churches (to be one up on the others) called themselves "All Saints" or "All Angels" and tried to grab the lot, but in fact, we know that we do not claim the particular protection of saints or angels. They are God's messengers, not ours – at least not yet ours. They will be one day, but not now. We go straight to God through Jesus Christ and him alone.

Having cleared the decks of those matters, let me begin to say that the Bible teaches that angels are a distinct order of beings, between mankind and God. Not mediators, they are an order of creatures superior to people and inferior to God. They are superior to us because they are stronger than we are, they are more beautiful than we are, and they are more intelligent than we are. They are not born as we are born; they do not grow up as we grow up; they are not married as we marry; they do not have children as we have children – so their number is fixed by God, who made them. He created them and they have stayed that way since.

They are spirits and they do not have bodies of flesh, though they do have the power to appear as bodies. They do not die as we all die. They belong to heaven, not earth, yet they are inferior to God. They do not share his power or his knowledge. He alone is almighty, and he alone is all knowing. They are not eternal, there was a time when they were created, and so God himself is the only eternal being.

There are countless numbers of angels in the universe. "Ten thousand times ten thousand" is one phrase; "myriads upon myriads"; and "hosts" — do you notice how that word "host" goes through the Bible? There is the captain of the Lord's host; and there is the God of hosts. The word "host" is the biggest number of people you can get in the Hebrew language. There are titles, grades, ranks and names among them; there are archangels, cherubim, seraphim, principalities, and powers. Some of them are named— Gabriel, Michael, and Lucifer are mentioned within the pages of scripture.

We are told that their beauty is such that, if we saw them in their heavenly glory, we would say, "How utterly beautiful." Artists and sculptors have found the human form very beautiful, but if we could see the angels we would say, "Now that is real beauty." Their strength is as Jacob discovered it to be one night as he wrestled with an angel by the brook. He wrestled and wrestled, but he finished up lamed by the angel. One angel, as we shall see, is more than a match for 186,000 foot soldiers of men.

Consider their intelligence—they are not omniscient, they don't understand everything, but they are far more intelligent than people. They know what is happening on earth; they know what is happening in your life. Much more than anyone else, the angels know. They do not know the date of our Lord's second coming, but according to the Bible, they know many other things. Their speed! How they can travel! Perhaps this is what the phrase "six wings" means.

On one particular day, Daniel prayed to the God of heaven. God dispatched from highest heaven an angel and said, "Go to Daniel's bedroom." The angel was standing there before Daniel finished his prayer. If you read his prayer aloud in Daniel, you discover that it lasted less than one minute, yet the angel travelled from highest heaven and was there with Daniel in his bedroom when he finished, so swiftly can the messengers of heaven fly to do God's bidding. Why is it that you pray every time you come to church or whenever we say the Lord's Prayer, "Your will be done on earth as it is in heaven?" You are saying "May I be as quick to do your will as the angels do it; may I run to do it; may I go swiftly to give your message to someone who needs it."

Perhaps the most important thing the Bible says about the angels is that there are good ones and bad ones in the proportion of two to one – that a third of the angels of heaven have rebelled against God and have decided to try to take his kingdom from him. More about that later. For now we will think about the good ones and what they did in the ministry of Jesus. Not only were they there at his birth – conducting those very delicate negotiations with Joseph and Mary; bringing those startling messages to human beings – but all the way through the ministry of Jesus you discover the angels are stepping in at point after point.

When he was tempted and alone with the wild beasts and the devil in the wilderness, who helped him through that? We are told that the angels came and ministered to him – they came to support him. There was one occasion when Jesus was going through a village and people were rude to him, shouting, "Get out of our village, we don't want you!" The disciples said, "What shall we do? They deserve fire from heaven. Shall we pray for that?"

Jesus said, "Don't you realise that I have ten thousand angels just waiting to do what I tell them? If I wanted to blot anyone out, I would just call the angels to come. They would deal with them." Ten thousand angels followed Jesus through his Galilean ministry and he could have called on any of them at any moment.

Go to the garden of Gethsemane—once again he was all alone. The disciples were asleep. Who helped him through that dreadful agony when the drops of sweat became his blood on his brow? The angels came and ministered to Jesus.

There was only one crisis in our Lord's life when the angels did not come and help, and that was when he was all alone on the cross. Then there was not an angel in sight. The sun had gone out; God had departed; the God of light had gone and gross darkness came over the earth for three hours. An angel could have pulled the nails out. An angel could have blasted those priests and those Jews and Romans to eternity as easily as we speak, but no angel came— there was no help. The legions of angels were silent and stayed away.

But who rolled away the stone from the tomb? No human being touched that stone. One angel came down and it is estimated that the stone weighed a ton and a quarter, and an angel rolled it, pushed it over and sat on it, according to the Bible. That is the strength of an angel. When the bewildered disciples came they said, "Where is he? Where has he gone? Where is the body?" and it was angels who conveyed the message: don't look for a living Saviour in a cemetery. "He is not here. Why seek the living among the dead? Go and tell the disciples he will see you in Galilee."

When the moment came for Jesus to go back to heaven – as they stayed gazing up into the clouds, angels came. They said, "Why are you still looking up into heaven? He has gone,

17

but he is coming back in the same way. Now you go back into Jerusalem and wait as he told you." I defy anyone to make sense of the biblical account if they rule out the presence of angels. They would be left with insuperable problems, of which the rolled away stone is just one.

Now just pause for a moment—the angels, until Jesus' birth, had always looked up to him. He was on the throne of glory in highest heaven. Now, to their amazement, they are looking down. For the first time ever, they have to look down to see the Son of God. No wonder they said, "Glory to God in the highest and on earth peace, goodwill toward men." They saw the Son of God, a little baby in the manger. Now Jesus is back above them and they see him where he was originally, yet they see him differently. For the first time they see the Son of God above them with a human body. Now they look up to a man. The man who was lower than the angels is now high above them – the pioneer preparing our place – for one of the secrets of the Bible is that, though the human race is below the angels now, those who believe in Jesus will share his superiority to the angels, and one day the angels will do what we tell them. That is the destiny of every Christian believer—to have the angels at our bidding one day. That should make us gasp with astonishment. Let me bring it down to earth: next time you are pushed around by the boss in the office or the factory, just say to yourself, "I'll one day have legions of angels under me." That might just relieve you and might just help you to get a true perspective. It may sound like appealing to the old Adam, but I don't think so. Just remember your destiny and it will make you behave as a royal son, prince or princess, someone destined for glory.

So we have seen the angels' ministry to Jesus, one of whose titles is "Captain of the Lord's host". What about their ministry to human beings?

Jesus spoke of the interest of the angels in little children. Every time you look after a little child, every time you try to talk to a little child about Jesus, there is an angel listening. Teachers and Sunday school teachers need to be aware of this. Jesus warned: "Beware what you do with these little children. Their angels behold the face of my Father in heaven."

So one of their tasks is to report on what you do with little children. When one thinks of the cruelty to body, mind and soul that is done to little children, one thinks that some people are going to face an awful retribution when the angels bring their reports. You see, Jesus is saying that what you do is known to angels and will therefore be reported, so beware – take heed lest you offend one of these little ones.

He also said that if just one person repents of sin and accepts Christ as Saviour, the angels in heaven will start singing; they will sing their heads off. This means that the angels are watching services. They know all about what is going on. They know you are present. The hosts of God are around us when we worship. If one person goes out of your church meeting believing in Jesus, who came into it a sinner and who did not know the Saviour, the angels are going to be talking about it: "One sinner repented and has come into the family."

The Bible testifies to the ministry of angels in many ways towards the people of God. The first is *the ministry of surrounding a person with a wall of protection* against danger, terror and that which we might fear. Jacob was all alone the first night away from home. I know what that is like. Do you remember the first night you were away all on your own somewhere, in a strange bed, feeling homesick and lonely? Jacob was lying out in the open air. Having had to run away from home, he did not even have a house to stay in. As he looked up in the sky he thought of Esau, his brother, who might come running after him to do him harm. He slept, he dreamt, and he saw angels going up and down just where he was.

As a child I was taught to think of angels by my bed. I am afraid I dismissed that when I grew up, and I thought, "Well, what a silly idea. Angels by my bed, that's like fairies down in the garden." But now I know it is true. Now I know that you can go to bed and you can say, "O God of hosts, guard me while I sleep." Jacob woke up and said: this is none other than the house of God, the gate of heaven; I'm right there, and these angels are all around me, coming and going all the time. He didn't see them when he woke up, but he knew they were there and that wherever he went he would know that protection.

Israel knew that protection—there came a terrible, dark night in Egypt where death came to every home, but the angel passed over each home of the people of God, and death passed over. We find that protection later, in the life of Elisha. I love the account of Elisha, especially when Elisha was not worried about the enemy round about. They were on the hill of Dothan, and the servant woke up in the morning, looked out and said, "Master, what shall we do? We're completely surrounded, they've come for you." Elisha said, "It's all right. O Lord, let the young man see what the real situation is." When he looked again, between the outer circle of the Syrians and Elisha the man of God, there was another circle of God's chariots. As the Syrians advanced towards Elisha, the angels touched the eyes of the Syrians and they could not see. The whole situation was saved—that was the ministry of protection.

Let me be right down to earth again. I remember hearing of a commercial salesman in a hotel who struck up an acquaintance with another salesman who was an ungodly man. The latter one said, "Look, let me go out and get a couple of girls for us for the night." The one who was a Christian said, "I don't want any girls." The other said, "I'm going out to get two and I'll come back for you." The Christian knew what temptation could be, and so he prayed for the God of hosts to protect him.

The man came back with a couple of girls he had picked up from the street, and they came into the dining room where the Christian was sitting. They looked all around the dining room, which had only a few people in it. They could not see him, and they went out and left.

The next day, the unbelieving salesman said, "Where did you get to last night?"

"I didn't go anywhere," came the reply.

"Well we came back to the dining room and you weren't there."

"Ah, but I was there."

"Well we didn't see you."

The hosts of God can still blind. They can still so control an unbeliever that he can't see the man he has come to drag away into sin. We can claim that protection. We can ask the God of hosts to be around us.

Who shut the lions' mouths in Daniel's den? I was brought up on the idea that they didn't eat Daniel because most of him was backbone and the rest was grit, but I do not think that is borne out by scripture. It tells you that an angel came and shut lions' mouths. Can you imagine that? An angel strong enough to hold the jaws of the king of the jungle together! It was not that the lions were peaceful and quiet and just lying around Daniel, as Sunday school pictures portray. They wanted to eat him up. They were hungry; they were savage, but you can't eat anyone when someone is holding your jaws tight shut. An angel came and held the jaws tight shut. The angels of God can protect you.

Angels can also *provide* for you. In the accounts of Hagar

and Elijah we see that angels can cook. Both were in the middle of the wilderness with nothing to eat, and they would have died unless someone brought them food. No-one knew they were there. In both cases an angel came and prepared food and drink for them, providing for them—that is an amazing thing.

Then there are angels who *punish*. Sodom and Gomorrah had the sort of life that would fill our tabloid newspapers. It was just two angels who came. They said, "We're coming to see for God what's going on. We have come to destroy these cities before God." Angels can destroy in God's name.

It was angels that barred Adam and Eve from the Garden of Eden, that lovely spot. We now know the location. We can put it on a map. It is in the valley where Tabriz is now situated, where fruit trees still grow. We know exactly where it was, but there was a man and his wife who could not get near that place because two angels stood there. Wherever they came the angels came, and said, "Away, away. God doesn't want you in here any more."

The Assyrians who came against Jerusalem came in their might—186,000 men armed, and little Israel was besieged inside Jerusalem. They prayed to God, and God sent just one angel. In modern times an archaeologist, digging around the cities of southern Judah, came across the grave of these Assyrians. There are literally thousands of skulls piled up. The archaeologist was looking at the work of just one angel. For God warned those Assyrians, "Come against my people, you come against me." He had told them, he had given them ample warning, and they persisted.

In the New Testament too, you find the same ministry. You find the *ministry of deliverance*. Here is a disciple of Christ chained in the inner prison with four guards and then a locked gate – but what is a padlock to an angel? An angel is marvellous for picking locks. Peter woke up in the middle of the night – an angel had opened the chain, which had gone. The angel said, "Shh, quickly, get dressed. Come on." Out they went, past the guards who were fast asleep. They came to the barred doors and, as they walked towards them, the doors opened. Peter made his way to the Christians who were having a prayer meeting. They were all praying, "Lord, get Peter out of prison."

Then there was a knock at the door, the maid went and she came back, and told the group, "It's Peter!"

They said, "It can't be. We're praying for him, he's in prison." They just couldn't believe it, but you see angels can get a man out of prison. You can't withstand an angel.

There is a *ministry of comfort*. When Paul was on his way, on that long, dangerous sea voyage, to face Caesar, an angel came to him in the night and said, "It's all right. You'll get there. You'll see Caesar. You'll be able to talk to him about the gospel."

You find a *ministry of guidance*. Philip is guided by an angel of the Lord to go to Azotus and first of all to go to a man who is the Chancellor of the Exchequer of Ethiopia, a man who is seeking God and reading the Bible. Philip is told by an angel to go, Cornelius is told by an angel to send for Peter – so I could go on.

I have heard so many stories in recent years of angels protecting, delivering, and providing for God's people. The interesting thing is that in most of the stories that I have heard, the Christians themselves did not see the angel. I will just content myself with two stories, one of which is told in a missionary book by Eberstein. He tells of how two missionary ladies in China, before the communists came, went to the town to get the wages from the bank for the hospital staff, were delayed in their journey back to the mission hospital, and had to spend the night out on the hills without protection. They had the money bag between them, and there were bandits in those hills who roamed by night, stealing and killing.

The two ladies lay down, put the money bag between them and said, "O God of hosts, protect us," before falling fast asleep. The next day they got safely home to the hospital. A few months later, a bandit was carried in with shotgun wounds. One of these ladies was bandaging him up when he said, "I know you, I've seen you. Were you not out on the hills one night?"

"Yes," she replied.

"Well," he said, "If it hadn't been for those soldiers, I would have come and taken whatever you had. I would have killed you."

She asked, "What soldiers?"

"Those twenty-four soldiers that you had with you."

"Twenty-four soldiers? No, there weren't any soldiers with us."

"There were, we counted them," he said.

A few weeks later that lady came home on furlough to her London church, and she told this story there. The church secretary, who was very methodical, said, "Can you tell me when that was?" She told him the date and he looked up his diary where he kept a record of how many came to the church prayer meeting. He said, "How many did you say? Do you know that very night there were twenty-four people here praying, we had a real sense that you were in danger, and we prayed that God would protect you."

The other story, from the Afghan Border Crusade, is almost humorous. In the times of the Bible, of course, angels rode chariots because they were the vehicles used then, but they ride bicycles today. A missionary who had to cycle from one town to another alone knew that it was one of the most dangerous roads from the point of view of human attack. So the missionary set out, again committed himself to the Lord, and arrived safely, but met a very evil man in the marketplace a few days later who again said to the missionary, "You know, if there hadn't been those others riding with you – I was waiting to kill you just two days ago."

"There were no others riding with me."

He said, "There were. What about all those other fifteen bicycles?" There they were, riding down the road in Afghanistan, and again the missionary was quite unaware.

Indeed, it is probably good for us that we don't know that there are angels all around us. We might get a bit big-headed; we might get false ideas. Just supposing how you would feel, walking down the high street, seeing a bunch of angels all around you. I think you would not be adapted to normal life. I think you would get put off balance emotionally. Sometimes it is necessary for us to see them, sometimes it is not, but we can claim their presence. We can go to bed tonight saying, "Send angels to guard me while I sleep." You can get up tomorrow morning, and whatever danger or responsibility you are facing, whatever you are afraid of, you can say, "O God of hosts, encamp around me, because I fear you." If you fear God, you fear nothing and no-one else.

I will tell you this: one day we are all going to meet the angels. One day you will believe in them, you will see them, because one day you are going to die. Then I will not be able to help you and your family will not be able to help you. One day you are going on a journey by yourself. There is a story in the Bible of a poor beggar. His name was Lazarus, which means a man who loves God. Nobody else loved him, he had nothing to eat and nowhere to live, and he lived on the pavement all by himself. He would have loved the crumbs that the rich people used to use to clean their hands. They didn't use serviettes, they took a piece of bread and they rubbed their hands clean on the bread and threw it under the table. He would have loved to have eaten that, but he couldn't and he died. The man whom no-one had cared for all his life was carried by the angels to Abraham's bosom.

The day will come when you take your journey alone, when human beings cannot help you any more. God has the angels waiting on the other side. They will show you around. They will take you where you need to be. One day the Lord Jesus is coming back from glory and everybody, the whole world, will see him; they will know that he is Lord, but I am told at least three times in the Bible that when he comes he is going to come with his angels, and we will see them with him. We will know they are real and we will know they are true and so will everyone. Isn't it thrilling to believe in angels and know that they really do exist? They are God's messengers and he sends them to help us and serve our needs if we belong to him.

2

BAD ANGELS

First, please read Ephesians 6:10 – 20. I know a Christian man who will not go out in the morning until he has put on the whole armour of God. Before he goes out of the front door, he stops and says, "Have I got my shield? Have I put my breastplate on? Did I put my helmet on this morning? Have I got my sword?" He deliberately runs through it, step-by-step, and he puts on each piece of armour, and then he goes out to meet the day. It is not surprising that he is not often defeated.

Ephesians 6:12 tells us that we are not contending against flesh and blood, but against the principalities, against the powers, against the world rulers of this present darkness, against spiritual hosts of wickedness in the heavenly places.

There are three surprises you get when you read the Bible in relation to our subject of angels. Number one is that there are such beings, angels—other intelligent creatures in the universe, supernatural, beyond our senses, superhuman.

The second surprise is to discover that there are bad ones as well as good ones. If, as you were reading the previous chapter of this book on good angels, you felt comforted and strengthened with the thought of good angels around you, I am afraid that you may well get rather mixed feelings as you realise that there are spiritual hosts of wickedness all around us too.

The third surprise is that these bad angels are not in some underworld; they are in heavenly places. That is where all the angels are anyway, and the bad ones are there as well as the good ones. The real battle that is going on today is not on earth at all, it is in heaven, and it is the bad angels in heaven who lie behind most of the troubles that we are having in this old world of ours.

This is the real answer to the old question "Where did evil come from?" The Bible makes it quite clear that it did not originate with God. When God made everything with his hands, he looked at it and said, "That's good, that's very good." Only good things could come from a good God, so evil did not come from him. Let us get that absolutely clear. But evil did not originate with man either. We are not that original, we got it from somewhere else. There is evil in nature as well as in man, and it would seem to me that man is not responsible for all the evil in nature. Some of it, yes, but not all of it. Mankind may be responsible for the deserts of dust that are the result of agricultural policies, but we are not responsible for many of the terrible natural disasters that occur.

Where then did evil come from? The Bible seems to state that evil began not with God, not with man, but among the angels, and that, because of their supernatural power, they have been able to corrupt this world in which we live, not only at the human level but at the level of nature too. Now there is not much written in the Bible about how evil began among the angels, because it was not written for speculation. It was written for the main purpose of facing human beings with their responsibilities. Therefore, it is not important for you to know all that goes on among the bad angels. You only need to know about them insofar as they can influence your life for evil, you don't need to know a whole lot of other things. But piecing together the hints there are in the Bible, we can say two things about the bad angels.

If we turn to the little letter of Jude, for example, we are told that the angels did not keep their proper place but left their proper dwelling. What does that mean? Then Peter, in his second letter, wrote, "The angels, when they sinned...."

There are two things about the angels that come from those two texts. One: the angels had free will. They were messengers, not machines. They could say, "God, I will not do what you want me to do. I will not take this message for you; I will not fulfil this mission."

The second thing that becomes clear is that they fell from their position of obedience. So the free will and the fall of angels is taught clearly in Scripture, and that is where they came from. They are not, of course, called angels when they fall, they are then called demons.

It is a tragedy that the very word misleads us because it is a word that evokes this kind of picture. I had a parish magazine pushed through my door today, and I always find it very interesting, but one of the illustrations in it depicted medieval demons – horrid little creatures boiling people up in cauldrons, stirring them with pitchforks, with all kinds of other lurid details. It was quite a bloodthirsty painting. We have inherited that kind of picture, but the word "demon" literally means "inferior deity" – someone nearly as powerful as God, but not quite; someone below God, and yet above us, and we must take demons very seriously.

How many are there? I don't know how many angels there are altogether. If I knew that, I could tell you, because there is an indication in Revelation 12 that one out of every three angels, became a demon, set himself against God, and is working against the kingdom of God. Frankly, that must mean millions. It is possible for such demons to get hold of a human being and possess them. Saul is a good example in the Old Testament, and Mary Magdalene is an example of a woman in the New Testament—human beings who have been taken over.

It is quite extraordinary that science fiction is now

producing the same kind of idea – things that can come from outer space and inhabit the bodies of human beings. Long before science fiction writers thought of that, the Bible was talking about possessed people. Let me say straight away that it is still (and pray God, always will be) a minority of cases, but it is possible to meet it in England today. It is more possible to meet demonic possession if you go overseas. In Southeast Asia, you will be up against this the whole time. If you go to any country where spirit worship is common you will see it, and of course spirit worship is becoming increasingly common here.

In our Lord's earthly ministry, he met people who were possessed by demons on at least six different occasions. There was an unclean spirit possessing one man; a blind and dumb spirit possessing another; there was a legion of spirits possessing the Gadarene demoniac; there was a dumb spirit; there was a girl, and there was a little boy. I was brought up on the interpretation that demon possession in the New Testament was simply their way of talking of mental disease, physical handicap, epilepsy or insanity. I now know that demon possession is completely different from a mental or a physical condition. The symptoms are different; the treatment is different.

For example, the symptoms of demon possession are these: (i) Supernatural strength, so that it may take nine or ten people to control the person physically, whereas in even the most severe mental case two or three strong men would be sufficient; (ii) Clairvoyance – a knowledge of other people that is quite impossible to have except by supernatural revelation; (iii) An ability to use voices that are quite different from the person's own voice; (iv) A profound antagonism to the name of Jesus; (v) A wild reaction to prayer so that a possessed person will go berserk when prayer is offered. Those symptoms that belong to demon possession are quite different from the most advanced case of schizophrenia, or the most serious case of physical handicap.

Furthermore, the cure is quite different. Demon possession is cured very quickly indeed – in a matter of hours at the most, but often in a matter of minutes through the power of Jesus and through the power of the name of Jesus – whereas a mental condition is not cured instantaneously, but requires lengthy therapy of different kinds.

When Jesus met demon-possessed people, they recognised him, saying, "Get away from us. We know who you are. You are the Holy One of God." The demons were the first to know who he was. In every case, he dealt with that demon on the spot and liberated the person from possession. Whether the symptoms were physical, mental or spiritual, he was able to deal with them quite quickly.

Not only did Christ meet these cases, but he also commissioned his disciples to fight them. I think of the moment when they went out, two by two, having been told by Jesus that they must cast out demons as well as heal the sick. I can imagine them being terribly afraid of meeting someone who was demon-possessed and finally doing so, and one of the disciples saying to another, "Well you do this one and I'll do the next," and, "No, you first. I'm sure you could do it better than I could," and trying out the name of Jesus in that situation, and discovering to their delighted astonishment that "Jesus is the name high over all in hell or earth or sky, angels and men before it fall, and devils fear and fly."

In Acts we find that Peter, Paul and Philip met such situations, and in the power of Jesus dealt with them. We can also see in the New Testament something of the aims of the demons. What are they trying to do? The answer is two things—to deceive people and to destroy them. This is the aim of every demon: to deceive you until your thinking is crooked, until you cannot see straight, until you cannot see the truth; to delude you, to twist you and then to destroy you – either to destroy you physically, throwing you off a cliff or into the fire, or to destroy you mentally; to destroy you morally; to destroy you socially until, like the Gadarene demoniac, nobody dares come near you; or to destroy you spiritually. They are out to deceive and to destroy everyone they can get hold of, and they will do so.

It was Jesus who said that he prayed for his disciples that the evil powers would not get hold of them. Now just as the Bible in talking of good angels talks about God, their leader, much more than good angels, so the Bible talks much more about the leader of the bad angels than the demons themselves. It tells us a whole lot about a person called Satan, the devil. Our Lord Jesus is given two hundred and fifty names and titles, but the devil gets five names and twenty-four titles, more than any other person in the New Testament apart from the Lord Jesus. Therefore, it behoves us to look at what is said. Satan was the first to say to God, "No. I will not be part of your kingdom. I want a kingdom of my own," and he went to the other angels and said, "Will you come with me? Don't have this God over you" – and the demons are those who said yes.

This important and powerful angel of hell, whom Ezekiel tells us was the anointed cherub nearest to the throne of God, is the one we call Satan. I want to underline that. You can be as near to God as that and you can rebel; the nearest to the throne of heaven, he said no to God. Here are his five names: Satan; Abaddon (which is *Apollyon* in Greek and means destroyer); Beelzebub; Belial and Lucifer. Every one of them is a horrid name. There is nothing sweet about those names, either in their meaning or their sound. Here are some of the adjectives: subtle, wicked, unclean, evil, lying and, above all, proud. That is a horrible description of a character, and it is the last one that comes out most.

He is described in terms of animals. He is likened to three in particular, and two of them come from the reptile family, which is interesting – in a zoo I have a kind of morbid curiosity when I enter the reptile house. The devil is described as a wily serpent, a snake in the grass, subtle, clever, a red dragon, cruel, powerful; then he is described as a prowling lion, a roaring lion, king of the jungle.

I remember a train I took from Mombasa to Nairobi in Kenya. The journey, on a single track line, took all night as the train wound its way up to the plateau – to the White Highlands, as they were called. I remember reading the story of how that railway was built; how half the builders had to wait with guns while the other half laid the sleepers and tied the rails to them with spikes, because of the lions all the way up, kings of the jungle who lay in wait. Many lives were lost just to get that single railway line up to Nairobi built, because of the prowling lions all the time. When you go out of your church meeting you will be followed by a prowling lion, and if that were the case physically – if there literally was, to your knowledge, a lion loose in your town – and you knew that it was prowling around the streets, you would be on your guard. The Bible uses this picture of the devil to tell you: watch it, there is a prowling lion in your town, and he is after you, so be on your guard. It is interesting that the Holy Spirit is likened to a dove. What a contrast – you will have seen a little white dove fluttering down. God knows what he is doing when he uses animal metaphors in the Bible.

Now look at some of the activities of the devil. He is a slanderer, a tempter, a deceiver, an accuser, a tormentor, a murderer and a destroyer. If a human being could have all that said about him, he would be in court straight away, yet this person is on the loose.

He is a *slanderer*, he loves to slander, and whenever we slander people the devil is using our mouths. He is a *tempter*, playing on the desires of our flesh. One of the texts in the Bible about this says that he plays us like fish. Have you ever seen a fisherman choosing his bait, knowing just what to use, and then playing the fish? "I know how I'll get him. He's down there. I'll just play this above him." The devil is doing just that when he lures and entices us. That is the phrase in James 1 — he lures us, entices us out, and we just follow along.

Billy Graham, in one of his sermons, talked about a farmer trying to get his pig to market and discovering that, with a pig, if you drive it one way it goes another way. The farmer eventually found that if he laid a trail of beans, the pig just came right along to the slaughterhouse, picking up one bean at a time and following along. The devil is a master at doing that – dropping something in front of you that you would like, and another thing and then another thing, and along the track you go.

He is the *accuser*—he is the self-appointed counsel for the prosecution; *tormentor*—he can cause you physical pain. Paul had a messenger of Satan in his flesh to torment him; a physical handicap that he had to battle with all his life and ministry.

I think it is the titles of the devil that worry me most. He is the *prince of this world*, the *ruler of this world*, and as Jesus called him, *the god of this world*—the only person Jesus ever called "god" apart from his own Father. He was teaching that the devil is the one that people really worship, though they do not know it. He is the one that they really bow down before, and they are just not aware of it.

You know, that explains why news media are so full of stories of trouble. Do you remember a television bulletin that was all good news? Why is the world in such a mess? What is the explanation? We have sincere, gifted people trying to put it right. We have people of goodwill who want a good world for their children. Why can't they achieve it? Why will we never get there? Why can't we get any nearer? I'll tell you why: because the real person who is running this world is the devil. As the prince of this world, he will make quite sure we don't get peace except on his terms, which will be totalitarian surrender. That is why we need to take him very seriously indeed.

On one occasion, he is described as *the prince of the power of the air*, and the air in the Bible is always taken to mean the part of heaven that is nearest to us and that surrounds us and, as it were, hems us in. In other words, between us and highest heaven is the arena of Satan, ringing the earth, the air all around us. That is where he is, the prince of the powers of the air, between us and the highest heaven. Now he is a king and he has a kingdom, and there are four words used in the Bible to describe that kingdom.

Firstly, it is a kingdom of *disobedience*. Everybody who is disobedient belongs to that kingdom. You were born into it; you grew up disobedient; you learned what it was to say "No" before you said "Yes"; you never had to be taught to be bad, only to be good; you never had to be taught to be rude, only to be courteous; you never had to be taught to be dishonest, only to be honest. You were born in a kingdom of disobedience. As Jesus said to those who would not believe in him, "You are of your father, the devil."

Secondly, it is a kingdom of *darkness*—moral darkness as well as physical. The darkness that there is in this world of ours, and the deeds that are done in the dark, because men dare not come to the light, are the deeds of the kingdom of Satan. Satan loves darkness, which is why those who are in his grip love to live in darkness rather than light. They will love to sleep during the day and live at night, whereas God's plan was that people should work in the day and sleep at night, while many beasts sleep in the day and come out at night. That is the plan of God in the Bible, but you will find when the devil gets hold of someone, they keep later and later hours. You begin to live in the darkness, not the light. It is amazing how the devil turns you around this way.

Thirdly, it is a kingdom of *disease*. Why are there hospitals? Why are there doctors? Why are there doctors and nurses who have to work to keep health services working around the clock? Why do we need medicines and surgery? It is because we are living in the devil's kingdom. God never intended sickness and disease. It is not his will. When they brought a woman to Jesus to be healed, he looked at her and said, "You see this woman? She has been bound by Satan these eighteen years." Paul had a messenger of Satan, a thorn in the flesh. He asked God, "Take it away, take it away," and God said, "No, in your case I'm not going to, because I think you can glorify my name even more by showing what grace can do with a messenger of Satan." He left Paul with the disease. Sometimes God cures a disease; sometimes he leaves it, but every disease is a messenger of Satan.

What about death? Every time you see a hearse go along the road, you are seeing something that Satan did. Death was never intended for human beings. We were never intended to have our relationships broken. Death is something that Satan has introduced to our world. God never intended the profession of undertakers, and they will be out of a job later. I remember reading this sentence in a book and it hit me so forcibly: "Every cemetery owes its existence to Satan."

That, then, is his kingdom. What is he aiming at? The answer is that he is trying to be God. He is trying to have a kingdom of his own. To everybody he whispers to he says, "Wouldn't you like to be like God?" From the garden of Eden onwards, "Wouldn't you like to be like God; control yourself, have your own kingdom, the power and the glory for yourself?" That is what he does. He got hold of

Nebuchadnezzar, who was strutting around the Hanging Gardens of Babylon, one of the Seven Wonders of the World. Nebuchadnezzar said, "Is not this great Babylon, which I have built by my mighty power as a royal residence and for the glory of my majesty?" Listen to it! Is not this my kingdom, my power, my glory, Babylon? A few months later that king was living like a beast, eating grass in the field – his fingernails were like claws, his hair was long and he had lost his sanity.

It is said in the book of Isaiah about the devil himself: "You said in your heart I will ascend to heaven above the stars of God. I will set my throne on high. I will sit on the mount of the assembly in the far north. I will ascend the heights of the clouds. I will make myself like the Most High," and anybody who talks like that, whether he is trying to build an empire in big business, or whether he is being the big boss in his own family; every man who is saying, "Mine is the kingdom," is a man whom Satan has got.

One day Satan said to Jesus, "All the kingdoms of the world I'll give to you." He was offering him the post of Antichrist. One day a man will take that post from Satan and become the ruler of the world. Satan can give you the world. He can give you the power; he can give you the glory and the kingdom. All the kingdoms of the world belong to Satan and Jesus did not contradict that. He didn't say, "They're not yours to give." He said, "Satan, I'm going to go on serving God, not you."

Young people, older people, men and women, may I say to you: the devil can give you the world. He can offer it to you and say, "I'll give it to you." If you take it, you are riding the back of a tiger, but he can give it to you.

So he became the enemy, the adversary of God's kingdom. Here are some of the things he does, according to my New Testament. He sows tares among the wheat. Wherever God's seed of the Word is sown, Satan comes and sows something else. He blinds the minds of unbelievers. Why is it that some of your unconverted friends and relatives won't listen to you? You talk to them. They need Christ, and you tell them this, and they are as blind, dumb and deaf as a corpse. What has happened? The answer is that Satan has blinded their minds and they cannot see.

He masquerades as an angel of light. He got hold of Judas and he nearly got hold of Peter. Out of twelve disciples, Satan got hold of Judas through his money. Jesus said to Peter, "Satan has wanted to have you, Peter." Of course he did. Peter was to be the first pastor of the church, and Satan wanted him badly. Jesus prayed for him against Satan, "I prayed for you that Satan should not have you." Even though Peter denied Jesus, Satan did not get him. Satan hindered Paul in going to Thessalonica. He instigated the persecution and the martyrdom of Christians. No wonder the Lord's Prayer includes the petition, "Deliver us from the evil one."

Now in conclusion, may I ask you this question? Supposing you say to me, as you well could, "I've never come across any evil spirits. I've never had any personal experience of the things you're talking about." I really do not know whether to be glad or sorry for you. I am going to tell you how you can contact evil spirits. You may say, "But I don't want to." That is true, but you are going to find them one way or another, and there is a wrong way to find them and a right way. Let me describe, first of all, the wrong way according to the Bible.

Here are some of the wrong ways. The most obvious way to get through is spiritism, which is gripping thousands of people. Many go for comfort, they go from the best of reasons—they have been bereaved and want to know: what is happening to my loved one; where are they; what are they doing? They go for comfort. One night I gave a lecture on spiritism. As soon as I came into the room, I knew there were spiritists present, even though I had not seen them. I felt them, and so did some of the believers present; and I know Christians were praying that night because there was a spiritual battle that went on between unseen powers.

There were two ladies there, and I asked them afterwards, "Why did you become spiritists?" They told me it was after bereavement and I said, "How long have you been with them?" and one had been twelve years. I said to her, "Did you really find comfort? Are you more peaceful now about the afterlife than when you joined?" She said, "Quite frankly, no." Of course you are not. If spirits could give you peace, they would lose you again. They want to keep you dangling on the end of uncertain messages that make you want more, and you are so easily hooked. You can so easily be led on by those beings down the line.

Spiritism – is there anything in it? Yes, there is. I remember going to see a widow whose sister had taken her along to a séance and she said to me, "Is there anything in it?" I said, "There certainly is." She said, "What a relief." She said, "I've asked one or two others and they have just laughed and said it is all fraud and chicanery." Then she asked, "It's alright for me to go, then?" I said, "No, it's all wrong. If there was nothing in it, it would be all right to go." There is fraud; there is chicanery; there is telepathy, but there is reality too. You can get through, and you can get messages that tell you things that nobody else knows in the world about you and about your loved ones, because the spirits know. It is absolutely forbidden to God's people to dabble. Leviticus 19, Isaiah 8, and Micah 5 are enough to tell you that. Indeed, in the Old Testament, a Jew caught dabbling in that was sentenced to death, so seriously was it regarded. Saul is the outstanding case. He had banished all mediums from the land at one stage. Then later, when Samuel died, he killed the priests and secretly began to visit the witch of Endor. When I visited the little village of Endor, I thought of a king stooping so low as to sneak, disguised, into the house of a medium to get messages. He got a message that he did not like and it finished in his suicide.

We can be delivered from this, because Jesus has more power than the spirits. We don't need to be afraid of them any more because Jesus is stronger than all of them.

Another way is through black magic and devil worship, usually done in secret and, notice, in darkness, with immoral rites and orgies attached, and often a kind of perverted reversed picture of Christian ceremonies: black mass instead of white mass and black communion instead of Holy Communion. I went into a newsagent's, looked along one shelf and there were five books on black magic and devil worship in Britain—that is the way it will come. We are not going to be wrestling against flesh and blood, but against principalities and powers, spiritual hosts of wickedness in heavenly places, and we need the whole armour of God.

Other ways in which people contact the spirits wrongly are through: astrology; divining of different kinds including water divining; soothsaying, horoscopes, "readings" (what happened to you because you were born on such and such a date and in the sign of this, that and the other). Don't have anything to do with such things, even as a joke. Don't read such things because you will treat them as a joke for so long and then one day something will be said that a demon put right there so that you will be convinced there is something in this and there is a little hook that has begun to get into your soul.

Idolatry is another way. Why is it wrong to bow down to idols and graven images? They are just blocks of stone and wood. They cannot do anything; they cannot speak or move. The answer, according to Paul, is that behind the idols are demons, and those who worship idols will have demons getting through. To eat meat offered to idols can lead you to have communion with devils, just as eating bread and wine with Christians can enable you to have communion with the Lord Jesus.

One of the favourite tricks of the devil is to plant within the church of Christ those who preach heresy, and he always plants the nicest possible people – kindly, friendly, who have taken the glorious gospel of Christ and just twisted it here and there. We are told in the New Testament again and again to beware of tickling ears that just want to hear some new teaching, some new theology, some new doctrine – because the devils love it.

Well then, let me come to the right way to get through. We *are* supposed to get through to them, but in the right way, and I will tell you how. As soon as your Christianity becomes supernatural, as soon as you break through into the heavenly places, you will meet them; as soon as your religion gets above the chapel roof and gets into the heavenly places you will be aware of a tremendous battle. Your prayer life will become a battle. You will become aware of evil forces fighting what you do.

In other words, it is because we are so ordinary and so mundane, and so down-to-earth in a sense in our faith, that we never get into the heavenly places where the battle is on. You can go to church without ever meeting an evil spirit. You can sing hymns, but if you are going to get into the front line you will meet them. Get into the prayer meeting, that is where you will meet the power of evil. Get into the front line of the battle. It is up there, and the nearer you get to Christ, the nearer you are to Satan. The nearer you are to God, the nearer you are to principalities and powers, and therefore it may be that our experience of these things is limited because we are not as near to God as we need to be.

To put it simply, when the Holy Spirit is really operating in your life, the evil spirits will be operating against you, but when the Holy Spirit is not operating, the evil spirits leave you alone; they have no need to bother. Why should they bother? I have been asked if taking drugs leads to spirit possession. My answer is, not of itself because quite frankly, I don't think a demon would be interested in a drug addict. A drug addict has already taken the step toward self-destruction and I think the demons would just say, "Let him destroy himself. Let him get on with it." The only danger there is that drug takers often try other things for kicks and try other things in the occult to get experiences, and therefore it often leads to the other, but of itself it doesn't.

But when we are living in the heavenly places, in the forefront of the battle, then we must expect to feel the presence of evil. When we do, there is only one simple thing to do, and it works. It is to say, "In the name of Jesus, go." They have no choice at all. Confronted with the authority of our Lord Jesus Christ, no demon or devil can say a thing or do a thing.

In the next chapter I want to describe for you the battle between the good angels and the evil angels, how it is all going to turn out, and the triumphant victory that we are promised in the New Testament.

3

CONFLICT OF
SUPERNATURAL POWERS

I want to try to tie together some of the loose ends that we have left. We have thought about the good angels of God. Maybe you began to think about them really seriously for the first time. You found great comfort in the thought that God is surrounding us with his ministers—his messengers. Then we looked at the bad angels, and perhaps discovered to your surprise that the bad angels are in heaven just as the good ones are, and that their dedicated task is to hinder the work of God and do everything they can to stop the kingdom being extended.

Indeed, I can illustrate the conflict between the two very simply, in an interesting way, from the book of Daniel. When referring to the good angels I mentioned that Daniel prayed to God (as recorded in Daniel 9). An angel left the throne of God at the beginning of Daniel's prayer and got into Daniel's room before he got off his knees. So swiftly do they move – right from the Father's throne in heaven to Daniel's bedroom in the space of a prayer so short that reading it takes only about two and a half minutes. But in the very next chapter an angel arrives and states that he has been delayed twenty-one days, and that not until Michael (another important angel of God) gave him help could he get through.

Now this may seem to some like fairy tales. It may sound incredible. Yet I introduce it this way to show you that there is a conflict going on in the universe. It is a conflict in heaven. It is a conflict between the angels who have remained faithful to the will of God, and those who have chosen to rebel against him. The universe is in a permanent state of war. Whether we as a nation are at peace or at war, every Christian is at war. That is why every believer is referred to as a soldier – not fighting other people, nor necessarily fighting social evils, though we are to fight those. But every one of us is a soldier because when we were saved we were put in the supernatural realm of the heavenly places, we are right in the thick of it, and we shall be in a permanent state of war.

Once we have grasped this, we have stumbled on the explanation of two puzzling facts. The first is the fact of outward conflict in the world. Why can we not stop the strife, the bloodshed and the war of the human race? To quote Churchill's fifth volume about World War Two, entitled *Triumph and Tragedy*, the subtitle is "How the Great Democracies Triumphed, and Thus Were Able to Resume the Follies that Had so Nearly Cost Them Their Lives". That is a Churchillian sentence, and it shows some understanding. No sooner do we get out of one than we begin to sow the seeds of the next. Why?

World War I was said to be the war to end war, and that such things were never to happen again. Within a quarter of a century we were in another bloody conflict. Why is it? Is it that mankind does not want peace? Surely there are enough people in the world who have goodwill and who don't want to fight. Why can we never attain what we are seeking, what many fought and died for? Why is this world in such a perpetual state of conflict that it is like the surface of a boiling cauldron, in which we do not know where the next bubble or trouble will appear.

The answer is that no war yet has defeated the real enemies. The conflicts of earth are an overspill. We may think that those who have caused war are a particular group of people and that if we can get rid of them we shall end strife. We never will. Even if you were to get rid of every group, every nation, every class whom you think responsible for the trouble, I guarantee that before long you will be in trouble again. The real enemies are not flesh and blood, they are the evil angels, the principalities and powers.

Now the second puzzling fact is the inward conflict which every Christian experiences. There is outward conflict, which everybody in the world knows about, and the inward conflict which only the Christian knows about. Is it not true that when we came to know the Lord we had a honeymoon period in which we walked on the mountaintops with him. We were amazed that life could be so wonderful and apparently so easy. We loved him, we loved others. Then the honeymoon was over and we found ourselves in a battlefield on the front line – just as during the war some of our men came home and married and had just a brief interlude and then were thrust back into the fight. Every Christian will tell you that very quickly he was in the front line again and battling hard to keep his feet.

Why? Look again at Romans chapter 7. Why is it that what I do is not the good I want to do? We want to do the will of God – then why can't we? What goes wrong? You will never realise what has gone wrong until you think of that conflict above, and your inner conflict is an overspill from it. To put all this in one word, the reason why the world is in such a state and the reason why you are is that we are in the devil's own territory. We are under his power; the world is his kingdom.

He's got the whole world in his hand is a lovely song, but I think you need to realise what you are saying when you sing those words. According to the New Testament, the truth about our world is that, "The whole world is in the power of the evil one." The whole world is in the devil's hands.

That is why we are where we are, and why we never seem

able to obtain what we most deeply desire in our heart of hearts. He has got the whole world in his hands—that is our trouble.

What is the way out of it then? The answer is to be found in the Lord's Prayer: "Lead us not into temptation but deliver us from the evil one." That is what our Lord taught his disciples to pray. Whenever we sing or pray that, we are asking that God in heaven will deliver us from the power that holds this whole world in its grip.

How does God deliver us? What is he doing about it? Well I want now to take you through the whole Bible "from generation to revolution" again, and these are good names if you think of them. I want to take you right through and show you that the scarlet thread that runs from cover to cover is the theme that God is delivering us, that God is our deliverer, our liberator, our Redeemer—same word — our rescuer, that he is our Saviour—that is why the Bible was written.

We will look briefly at the Old Testament and then, at greater length, the New. The Old Testament is a record of how God demonstrated to a certain people that he could deliver them from the grip of the most powerful enemy. He chose a remarkable people to do this – a small group of slaves who had no money, no property, no country, no resources, no army and no leader. These slaves, in the grip of the most powerful nation of the then known world, the vast Egyptian empire with its Pharaohs, whose pyramids still survive. God said, "I'll get you out of that. I'll deliver you," and he did.

With a mighty outstretched arm he brought them through. They called him a new name. They said, "You are the deliverer, you are the redeemer, you can save us." Against all the might of that nation, the slaves got out. Everywhere they went they faced the Jebusites, the Amalekites, the Canaanites, and all the other "parasites" as someone has said – the whole lot of them. Though they were facing superior numbers and superior weapons, God brought them through every time. There has never been such a thing in human history as the story of the Jewish conquest of the powerful nations. There is nothing like it in the annals of our race. No wonder then that when the emperor Frederick asked a philosopher, "Give me one proof of the existence of God" the latter's reply came as follows: "Your majesty, the Jews."

But that was only the first half of the Old Testament; the second half is just the opposite: that same nation of God is trampled on, overrun, occupied by one after another – Assyrian, Babylonian, Egyptians again, the Greeks under Alexander the Great, and finally the dreaded Romans. What had gone wrong? Why is it, in the first half of the Old Testament, victory, conquest; and in the second half, defeat; occupation? The answer is that God demonstrated to them not only that he could deliver them but that they also needed to be delivered from the evil one.

You see, what happened to the Jews when they were first delivered, given peace and plenty, is exactly what has happened to Great Britain following 1945. It is exactly what always happens when we are delivered from our physical enemies – we fall straight into the hands of our spiritual enemies. In the country of Israel there came that scrambling up to affluence. There came selfish greed and lust. There came that godlessness which has been a characteristic of our nation ever since we crowded the churches for national days of prayer in the war. That is what happened.

Though God saved the Hebrews from all their natural enemies, their supernatural enemies gripped them hard and they forgot their Maker. God needed to show them their real enemies. He had shown them he could deliver: "But now," he said, "I'm going to deliver you from these." He promised them that he would send them a deliverer to do that. The word in Hebrew of course is "Messiah" and in Greek it is "Christ".

47

Now we have got the setting to turn to the New Testament. You see the picture. A nation is occupied by Romans — and if you have never lived in an occupied nation I don't think you can appreciate what it is like to see foreign troops marching down your streets, fearing meeting one of them; to have a knock on your door. Most of us have not known this; if you have known it at all you will understand that the longing of the Jew was for liberation from the Roman boots, but when Jesus came he would not do it. If you want to know why the Jews refused their own deliverer, it was because he wanted to deliver them from their spiritual enemies. They wanted him to deliver them from natural enemies. But he said no, he had come to liberate them from evil. They wanted to be liberated from Romans. When would Jesus get on with the job? That is why the cross occurred.

Turning to the New Testament, we can refer to three things: the past defeat of our spiritual supernatural evil enemies, accomplished by the death of Jesus (see Colossians 2:15); the present defeat of the same supernatural powers of evil in our life today; and what God is going to do with them in the future.

Look at our Lord. Do you know the first mention of Jesus in the Bible? It comes in Genesis 3. God says to Satan, "I will put enmity between you and the woman and between your seed and her seed. He shall bruise your head and you shall bruise his heel." Here is the promise of God, stretching forward through centuries, that one day someone born of a woman would deal with Satan – not just cripple him, but deliver him a fatal blow. For thousands upon thousands of years the promise was left unfulfilled until one day a baby was born at Bethlehem.

Why was Jesus born? Read this passage of scripture: "Since, therefore, the children share in flesh and blood, he himself likewise partook of the same nature that through death he might destroy him who had the power of death, that is the devil, and deliver all those who through fear of death were subject to lifelong bondage."

To destroy the devil was Jesus' main purpose in coming – and to deliver people who were afraid to die. Of course they are afraid to die. If you are a citizen of the devil you will be bound to be afraid of that, if you even just think of its implications. I am meeting more and more people today, more than I have met in my ministry before, who are afraid to die, and Christ was born at Bethlehem to deliver them.

Here is another passage: "The reason the Son of God appeared was to destroy the works of the devil." Jesus came to destroy the evil spirits and take their power out of this world. There are very few people today who see that. Around Christmas time they might exchange Christmas cards, go to a carol service, but they never once realise that it was an invasion.

There were two old people, one just before the birth of Jesus and one after, who realised this. Think of Zechariah. If you have worshipped regularly in an Anglican church you may recognise these words: "Blessed be the Lord God of Israel, for he has visited and redeemed his people"; and it goes on: "To grant that we being delivered from our enemies," might do what? Enjoy peace and plenty? No! "serve him in holiness and righteousness all our days."

The other person was an old man called Simeon, and when he saw that baby he said, "Lord, now let your servant depart in peace according to your word, for my eyes have seen your salvation...." Salvation in that baby.

Think of the temptations—why is it that Jesus' first act in his ministry was a preliminary bout with the devil? Why is it that began in private and not in public? Because here you have got the two opponents meeting each other. The one who is the prince of this world, the devil, and the one who came to take the world from him: Jesus. When the devil said, "Look I will give you all the kingdoms of the world," Jesus didn't say, "They are not yours to give." They are his. Jesus did not accept the offer.

Think of Jesus' earthly ministry. Jesus was conscious all through his ministry of fighting not men and women (he never fought them) but fighting the supernatural powers of evil. That is why he said that if you are going to spoil the goods of a strong man you had better bind him up first. You had better be more powerful than he is or you won't get anywhere. He was saying that he has the power to spoil Satan.

"This woman, bound by Satan for eighteen years, shall I not loose her" – and he did. You see, he had the power to spoil the strong man's goods. Everywhere he went, he made commando raids on the kingdom of evil and set people free from the devil; set them free from demons.

People came to him one day saying that he did it by black magic, with the power of Beelzebub; that it was the devil who was making him do that. Jesus taught them: How dare you say that? Can a kingdom divided against itself stand? Can a house and family in a state of civil war stand? No, of course not. How can I take this victim of Satan and set him free by the power of Satan? It is a living contradiction.

One day he called his disciples and sent them out two by two, having instructed them that whenever they met a victim of Satan, they were to set them free. Imagine two of the disciples going down the road – James and John we could say – hoping that they will not meet anybody possessed with a demon. I wonder what they will do. Suddenly they meet someone possessed with a demon, in the grip of evil. James might say, "Well, you first John. You try this one and I'll do the next."

I wonder what they must have felt like when they came

to their first opportunity. I know what they felt like for their second. But for their first they may have said, "Well, what shall we do? Let's try it then, shall we? Let's get him somewhere private; here's a side street, let's get him there." Then they would have said, "In the name of Jesus," and the man was liberated. You can see the two of them rushing on to the second, can't you? When they came back to Jesus they said, "Lord, even the demons are subject to us in your name." Jesus looked up and he said, "I can see Satan falling like lightning from heaven." In their report he caught a glimpse of the final overthrow of this horrible creature.

Later, Jesus would say, "I'm going to go to Jerusalem," and Peter said, "You're never going to go there, Lord. They'll kill you if you go there." Jesus turned around and said, "Get behind me, Satan!" Why should Satan try to stop Jesus going to Jerusalem? Why should Satan try to stop him being killed? Surely this would be the answer. Surely it would achieve Satan's purpose that this Son of God should be removed from the earthly scene and help no-one else. Ah, but you see, we have missed the point. Satan knew that in the death of Jesus he would accomplish more victory than he ever had in his life.

Come with me into the upper room and listen to the things that our Lord is saying on the night before he is taken away. "Now is the judgment of this world. Now is the ruler of this world, the prince of this world, cast out. I, even I, when I am lifted up, will draw all men to me." He is excited because something is about to happen. He goes on to say to them, "I will no longer talk much with you. For the ruler of this world is coming but he has no power over me," and he goes to the cross.

"Having spoiled principalities and powers he made a show of them openly, triumphing over them in the cross." Jesus had spoiled the principalities and powers. He had taken this woman, that man, and that young person, and had liberated them, but now he was going to defeat the evil powers openly.

Was there ever such a show of evil as the cross? Was there ever such a demonstration for you to see of what the powers of darkness can do? They were so present that even the sun was blotted out and it became like midnight. The powers of darkness concentrated on one man, the man who was the Son of God, and he had to fight that last battle all alone, and even his Father left him alone to fight it. Jesus fought this battle with all the evil – not just of men, for you cannot just blame men for what was done.

What made man do such a terrible thing, the crowning disgrace of our history? It was because the supernatural evil spirits had got all of them in their grip, and because the powers of darkness were concentrated at one point in time and space, and one man fought them and won. When he said "It is finished" it was not a cry of despair but a cry of triumph. For the first time in the history of the human race one man had managed to do the will of God from his birth to his death, and all of the powers of evil had not been able to touch him.

This is why the cross has broken the powers of darkness, disarmed them, stripped them, for that is the word used in Colossians 2:15. As Jesus was stripped physically for the public to see, the evil spirits of the universe were stripped for you to see. As the veil of the temple was rent in two, and the dwelling of God was made open to men's gaze, so the veil covering men's eyes, blinding them to evil, was ripped away by the cross.

That is why the resurrection is so fitting and his ascension is so fitting. The Bible tells us that God not only raised Jesus from the dead but caused him to sit at his right hand, far above all principalities and powers, all the evil angels, the devil and his demons, and he is above them now. He fought them down here and won, and now he is above every one of them.

Think now of the present victory, which you can have. If what I am saying is true, you can prove it by a simple test. Next time you are up against the devil, resist him in the name of Jesus Christ who died on the cross. Do you know what will happen? The enemy will run, he will not dare stay. Here is James 4:7: "Resist the devil and he will flee from you."

That is proof that there is a man above who can give you the strength to do it. That is why you can have the victory. Again and again this comes in the Bible. Romans 16:20: "The God of peace will soon crush Satan under your feet." John says, "I write to you, young men, because you have overcome the evil one." How do you do it? John goes on to say that anybody born of God is kept by Christ and the evil one does not touch him.

When you say, "Lead us not into temptation," do you know what you pray for? There is a promise in the Bible that those who look to God will know that he will never let the devil or a demon tempt them more than they can bear, but will always give them a way of escape so that you need never for one minute in this life be under the control of the evil powers of the universe. That is why you pray, "Give us this day our daily bread" – you need that every day; "Forgive us our trespasses" – you need that every day. But you also need to go on every day: "Lead us not into temptation, but deliver us from the evil one" – and you will know that.

Finally, the Bible says, "We know that we are of God and that the whole world lies in the power of the evil one." Is the world going to stay there? Are the Christians the only ones who will ever know God's power over evil or is there something more?

There is, and I want to tell you what God is going to do to the evil angels. It is all there in the Bible. Everything is in God's hand finally, so we can sing "He's got the whole world in his hand." God knows what he will do about them. He has got a plan and he has revealed it. It consists of four steps, four things that he is going to do to the evil angels. Read the book of Revelation chapter 12 and chapter 20. In those two chapters you have a crystal clear picture of these four things. First: the devil and his angels are to be moved from heaven to earth. Second: they are to be moved from earth to a place called the "pit", which we will look at in a moment. Third: they are to be allowed to come back to earth for a very brief moment. Fourth: they are to be banished to hell. That is the picture. There will also be a step number five: there will be a new heaven and a new earth free from every trace of evil.

Have you been to Coventry Cathedral? As you go up the east steps, you see two grotesque statues stuck on the wall. Yet they have a message, and they are based on Revelation 12. Above you will see a statue of Michael, one of the most important angels of God. Cowering below, you will see that old dragon, that serpent, Satan himself, and that should remind you that one day God is going to tell Satan and all his angels to go down to earth for a time, but to get out of his heaven.

That is the first step and it says that there will be war in heaven and that Michael and the angels of God will fight Satan and his angels, and they will be banished to earth. They will be so angry and so frustrated knowing that their days are limited and numbered that they will pour out upon this world such evil as one hardly dare mention. When the world gets the full force of evil it is going to be in a terrible state. If God had not shortened the days there would be none saved.

Next step is to banish the devil from earth. One day, the earth is going to be free from war. One day, God is going to demonstrate in this world that there can be peace – when all things are under his control. That kingdom for which we pray in the Lord's Prayer will not be established by human effort. It will not be established by a "war to end war". It will be established when God banishes Satan from the earth, and then we will have peace – such peace that even nature will feel it, and the wolf and the lamb will lie down together and the lion eat straw like the ox.

After that comes the period when God shows what he can do with this world when the devil is out of it. The devil is allowed for one brief moment to come back (solely, to my mind, as far as I read the scripture, to show that even people who have enjoyed such peace can still be misled, and will be).

Then comes the great climax of all when Satan and all his angels, a third of the heavenly host that he dragged down with him, are cut out of heaven and earth and sent to God's garbage dump, for that is what hell is – never again to trouble the creatures that God has made. Hallelujah for that day! How we look forward to it – when the devil will never again touch us.

Somebody asked me whether the bad angels will ever be saved. The answer is quite clearly no. If you read Hebrews 2 it says that Christ did not die for the angels. The angels cannot be saved from themselves; we can be saved from their domination. They cannot be liberated from themselves. The bad angels are banished. The old heaven and earth that God made has been so contaminated and so spoiled that he wants to make a new one: "Behold, I make all things new." There will be a new heaven and a new earth.

My last question is this: where do you want to spend the next life? For our Lord said, "One day nations will be gathered before me. I will divide the sheep from the goats. I will say to these, 'Come you blessed of my Father, inherit the kingdom.' I'll say to those, 'You go to that place that is prepared for the devil and all his angels.'"

I think those who are rejecting God, and those who are living selfish, godless lives, and those who care not for these things, do not realise that they are choosing to live forever with the devil and his angels in hell. But those who believe in the Lord Jesus – and believe that he came to live to set people free, and to die to set us free from the bondage of sin and death that he might destroy the works of the devil, and enable us to live with God and his angels – want to sing of his mercies, that he should give any one of us the opportunity.

Angels may seem a bit unreal to some people. One day they will be terribly real to you. One day you won't question whether Mr Pawson knew what he was talking about. One day you will meet either the good ones or the bad ones face to face, and know that you will be living with them for evermore. If you are not living with the good ones it won't be anybody's fault but your own for you have heard the truth and the gospel is for everyone who believes. Jesus died to open the kingdom of heaven to all believers. Those are the words we say at many funeral services – and one day for yours.

Books by David Pawson available from **www.davidpawsonbooks.com**

A Commentary on the Gospel of **Mark**
A Commentary on the Gospel of **John**
A Commentary on **Acts**
A Commentary on **Romans**
A Commentary on **Galatians**
A Commentary on **1 & 2 Thessalonians**
A Commentary on **Hebrews**
A Commentary on **James**
A Commentary on **The Letters of John**
A Commentary on **Jude**
A Commentary on the Book of **Revelation**
By God, I Will (The Biblical Covenants)
Angels
Christianity Explained
Come with me through **Isaiah**
Defending Christian Zionism
Explaining the Resurrection
Explaining the Second Coming
Explaining Water Baptism
Is John 3:16 the Gospel?
Israel in the New Testament
Jesus Baptises in One Holy Spirit
Jesus: The Seven Wonders of HIStory
Leadership is Male
Living in Hope
Not as Bad as the Truth (autobiography)
Once Saved, Always Saved?
Practising the Principles of Prayer
Remarriage is Adultery Unless....
The Challenge of Islam to Christians
The Character of God
The God and the Gospel of Righteousness
The Lord's Prayer
The Maker's Instructions (Ten Commandments)
The Normal Christian Birth
The Road to Hell
Unlocking the Bible
What the Bible says about the Holy Spirit
When Jesus Returns
Where has the Body been for 2000 years?
Where is Jesus Now?
Why Does God Allow Natural Disasters?
Word and Spirit Together

Unlocking the Bible
is also available in DVD format from **www.davidpawson.com**

Lightning Source UK Ltd.
Milton Keynes UK
UKHW021034200420
361988UK00022B/1648